Mandala Coloring Journal
with Daily Affirmations

Written and Illustrated by
Laura L. Hallett

First Printing: 2018

ISBN-13: 978-1985563544

ISBN-10: 1985563541

Today I release the fear of being successful,
and I embrace the everyday proof of my magnificence.

Today I released the fear of being wrong,
and I embrace the joy of living my truth.

*Today I release the need to defend myself,
and I embrace my unapologetic confidence.*

Today I release those things which no longer serve me,
and I embrace freedom from clutter and confusion.

Today I release the fear of succeeding, and I embrace my journey filled with the joyous exploration of all of my abilities.

Today I release my fear and doubt, and
I embrace the truth that I am a Divine Creation.

*Today I release the need to self-sabotage, and
I embrace my ability to make healthy choices.*

*Today I release the need to push people away, and
I embrace balance in all of my relationships.*

*Today I release the need to control, and
I embrace the beauty of living in the question.*

Today I release the need to ask why, and I embrace
the clarity and wisdom of the Truth that flows through me at all times.

Today I release the need to say "yes," and
I embrace my undefended "no."

*Today I release the idea that I am unlovable, and
I embrace the Universal Love that flows through all.*

*Today I release the need to fit into anyone's boxes,
and I embrace a life lived fully out loud.*

*Today I release the shame I feel for the mistakes I've made,
and I embrace the truth that if I could have done better, I would have.*

*Today I release the need to play small, and I embrace
the greatness that has always been waiting for me to step into it.*

Today I release the fear of difficult relationships, and I embrace them as some of my greatest teachers.

Today I release the negativity of the unconscious mind, and I embrace the sweet moments of silence where I can always see the good.

*Today I release doubt and fear, and I embrace the Truth
I find available to me through my spiritual practices.*

Today I release old habits that have kept me stuck in the past,
and I embrace new, positive ones that transform my life.

Today I release the impatience I often feel, and I embrace the trust I have in the action of the Universal Intelligence within me.

*Today I release the need to replay situations in my mind, and
I embrace the forgiveness that allows me to let it all go.*

Today I release any appearance of illness or limitation,
and I embrace a healthy and happy lifestyle.

Today I release any negative energy I feel, and I embrace the transformation of it into love and light.

Today I release the negative experiences of the past, and I embrace the forgiveness of myself and others that sets me free.

*Today I release any ideas that lead to separation, and
I embrace unconditional love for everyone.*

*Today I release all blocks to achieving my goals, and
I embrace my path of success and fulfillment.*

*Today I release any hesitation or fear, and I embrace
each step that leads me to my amazing future.*

Today I release all excuses for letting life happen to me, and I embrace my determination to create a purposeful life of joy and peace.

Today I release all hurt, anger and resentment from my life, and I embrace each day with renewed enthusiasm.

Today I release all sadness and pain, and I embrace the loving grace of Spirit moving through me.

*Today I release that which keeps me from experiencing joy in my life,
and I embrace each day knowing it is filled with the greatest delights.*

Today I release the people I feel have hurt me, and I embrace the emotional freedom that forgiveness brings.

*Today I release all expectations, and I embrace the freedom
I have to live the life I've always dreamed of living.*

Today I release the need to control others, and I embrace everyone's individual right to create they life they want.

*Today I release the desire to hoard things, and I embrace
the ease and grace that comes from a clutter-free life.*

Today I release the chains that bind me to the past, and I embrace the path that allows new and wonderful relationships to enter my life.

Today I release the darkness that comes with despair, and I embrace the positive memories from my past relationships.

Today I release my regrets, and I embrace the lessons my past experiences have taught me.

*Today I release everything that gets in the way,
and I embrace my true path in life.*

Today I release what no longer works for me, and I embrace a state of balance and harmony throughout my daily life.

Today I release my chaotic monkey mind, and I embrace the brief periods of bliss and contentment I experience in meditation.

Today I release fear, anxiety, and any unstable emotions, and I embrace the moments of deep connection to my Sacred Source.

Today I release all my old patterns of fear and insecurity, and I embrace a life filled with joy and well-being.

Today I release the burdens of yesterday and the worries of tomorrow, and I embrace my present moment with a sense of passionate purpose.

*Today I release the belief in death, and I embrace
the Eternal Love that lives through me.*

Today I release the any internal turmoil I feel, and embrace the Peace that transcends all understanding.

Today I release the belief that I live in a world of limited resources,
and I embrace the amazing abundance of this vast Universe.

Today I release the need to limit myself to society's expectations of my gender, and I embrace both my feminine and masculine characteristics.

Today I release any experience of chaos, fear, or doubt, and I embrace the Peace that is always at the heart of my Being.

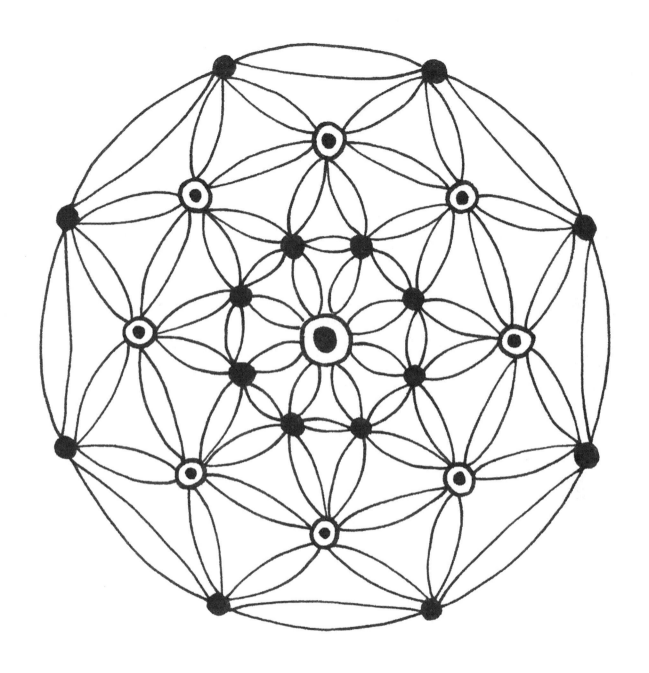

Today I release the belief that I am controlled by any prior circumstances or conditions, and I embrace each new day with bold confidence in who I've come here to be and what I have to offer the world.

*Today I release the unconditional Love that created me into the world,
and I embrace my connection with all Life.*

Today I release all the need to judge, to criticize, and be right,
and I embrace the wonder of the unknown.

Today I release _____,

and I embrace _____.

Today I release _____,

and I embrace _____.

Today I release _____ ,

and I embrace _____ .

Today I release _____,

and I embrace _____.

Today I release _____,

and I embrace _____.

Laura L. Hallett, B.S., M.Ed., MCS is a professional educator, curriculum designer, artist, and licensed minister with Centers for Spiritual Living (www.csl.org). She regularly speaks, conducts workshops, leads spiritual retreats, and teaches classes on meditation and transformational spirituality. For more information, check out Rev. Laura at www.laurahallett.com.

Made in the USA
San Bernardino, CA
08 June 2018